**TELL ME
ABOUT
ARTISTS**

# CLAUDE MONET

written by
**John Malam**

Evans

*Evans Brothers Limited*

Claude Monet was an artist. He painted in a new way that people were not used to seeing. At first, people were shocked by his paintings. He became very poor. But, slowly, people realised what a great artist he really was, and he became famous. This is his story.

A picture of Monet, painted by another artist called Renoir

Claude Monet was born on the 14th of November, 1840. He was born in Paris, the capital of France.

When he was five years old his family moved to Le Havre, a busy town on the north coast of France. His uncle and aunt, Jacques and Marie, lived in Le Havre. His Uncle Jacques owned a grocer's shop and Claude's father worked in the shop.

Paris in Monet's time

Claude went to school in Le Havre. He did not like school. When he was an old man he said: "School seemed like a prison and I could never bear to stay there, especially when the sunshine beckoned and the sea was smooth."

Le Havre today

When Claude was a teenager, his teachers found that he had a special gift – he could draw. Claude liked to draw funny pictures of his teachers.

He drew other people from Le Havre, too. An artist who lived in Le Havre saw Claude's drawings. He began to teach Claude about painting, and took him on trips to paint in the open air.

Claude's mother died when he was seventeen. By then he knew he wanted to be an artist.

One of Monet's funny drawings, made when he was 17 years old

But his father, Adolphe, wanted Claude to work in the family grocer's shop.

Claude asked his Aunt Marie for help. She made Adolphe see what a good artist Claude was becoming. So in the end, Adolphe said Claude could leave school and become an artist, if he really wanted to.

Monet painted this picture of his father and aunt sitting on their terrace in Le Havre.

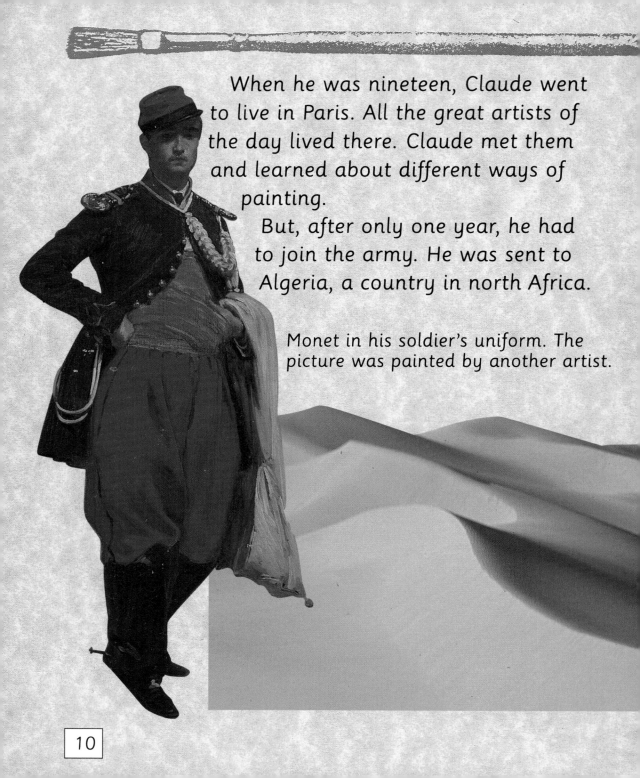

When he was nineteen, Claude went to live in Paris. All the great artists of the day lived there. Claude met them and learned about different ways of painting.

But, after only one year, he had to join the army. He was sent to Algeria, a country in north Africa.

Monet in his soldier's uniform. The picture was painted by another artist.

Claude liked the bright, clear light of Algeria. The sunlight sparkled and lit things in a way that he had never seen before. He began to wonder if he could paint as if the sun was shining on his pictures.

After one year in the army he became ill with typhoid. He was sent back to France to get better.

Once more, his aunt helped him. First, she paid for him to leave the army. Then, she persuaded his father to let him go back to Paris to paint.

Monet liked the bright, sunny light in the desert in Algeria.

In Paris, Claude joined an artists' studio. The other artists could see what a good artist Claude was. They liked him and he made many friends.

When he was twenty-five he had an accident. He hurt his leg and had to stay in bed. One of his friends found a way to keep water dripping on to his leg to help stop the pain. So Claude stayed in bed and painted at the same time!

When Monet hurt his leg, his friend painted this picture of him in bed.

Monet painted this picture of a stormy day at Le Havre.

For a long time Claude did not sell many paintings. He was very poor and did not have enough money to pay his rent.

His father and aunt became worried about him. They made him leave Paris. For a while, he lived in his aunt's summer house by the sea. He made a few paintings of the scenery around him.

In 1870, Claude married Camille Doncieux. Claude and Camille moved to London, to escape from a war that France was fighting. Claude did not want to join the army again.

In London, Claude painted the River Thames. He liked the way it looked in foggy light.

The next year Claude, Camille and their young son went back to France. At last Claude began to sell his paintings.

Monet painted this picture of his wife Camille a year after their wedding.

Monet called this picture of Le Havre 'Impression, Sunrise'.

Claude and his friends held an exhibition. One of Claude's paintings was called 'Impression, Sunrise'.

A writer who saw the exhibition did not like the paintings. He said they were only 'impressions'. To him, they looked like unfinished pictures, made in a hurry. From then on, Claude and his friends called themselves 'The Impressionists'. We still use this name today.

Claude liked to paint the same view over and over again. He painted Rouen Cathedral more than twenty times. He wanted to show the cathedral in different kinds of light.

Two of Monet's paintings of Rouen Cathedral. What differences can you see?

16

The Impressionist painters became well known. They held exhibitions and sold their paintings for large sums of money.

Claude moved to a big house near Paris. He decided to make a garden. He said: "What I need most of all are flowers, always, always." He even made a pond and grew water lilies.

Monet's house and garden

▶ Monet painted hundreds of pictures of his beautiful garden.

By now Claude was a famous artist. But he had many sad times. His wife Camille had died long ago. His second wife Alice died too, and then his eldest son died. Then he started to go blind. But he carried on painting until he died in 1926. He was eighty-six years old.

Today, people from all over the world buy paintings by Monet and the other Impressionist painters.

# Important dates

1840  Claude Monet was born
1845  Moved to Le Havre
1857  His mother died
1859  He went to Paris to train as an artist
1861  He joined the army and went to Algeria
1862  Returned to Paris to study art
1867  First son born
1870  Married Camille Doncieux
1870  Stayed in London
1871  His father died
1874  The first Impressionist exhibition was held
1878  Second son born
1879  Camille died
1892  He married Alice Hoschedé
1908  His eyesight started to fail
1911  Alice died
1914  His eldest son died
1926  Monet died

Monet in his studio

# Keywords

**artist**
someone who makes drawings and paintings

**exhibition**
a display of paintings for people to look at

**Impressionists**
the name given to an important group of artists whose paintings used light and colour to show how they saw the world around them.

**studio**
the place where an artist works

# Index